EVERY DAY SHOULD BE

Mother's Day

EVERY DAY SHOULD BE

Mother's Day

50 Ways to Honor, Appreciate,
Indulge, and Amuse Your Mom

Jennifer Basye Sander

Skyhorse Publishing

Skyhorse Publishing books may be purchased in bulk at special discounts for sales promotion, corporate gifts, fund-raising, or educational purposes. Special editions can also be created to specifications. For details, contact the Special Sales Department, Skyhorse Publishing, 307 West 36th Street, 11th Floor, New York, NY 10018 or info@skyhorsepublishing.com.

Skyhorse® and Skyhorse Publishing® are registered trademarks of Skyhorse Publishing, Inc.®, a Delaware corporation.

Visit our website at www.skyhorsepublishing.com.

10 9 8 7 6 5 4 3 2 1

Library of Congress Cataloging-in-Publication Data is available on file.

Cover design by Laura Klynstra
Cover image by gettyimages

Print ISBN: 978-1-5107-5233-7
Ebook ISBN: 978-1-5107-5234-4

Printed in China

Introduction

As I write this, I'm keeping an eye on the time as I have to remember to drive across town soon to pick up my no-longer-young mother for a doctor's appointment. I'm lucky (my mother is lucky, too) that I live somewhat close to my parents and that they are fairly healthy and still living in their longtime home.

When I was compiling *The Big Bucket List Book*, I spent months asking friends, colleagues, family, and sometimes total strangers, for ideas to include. I knew it couldn't just be a bucket list book of ideas that appealed to me. Likewise with this book: who wants to read a sappy book about all the grand and glorious things I do for my mother, or the touching and adorable things my nearly-grown children do for me? Instead, I spread the word far and wide in order to get fresh ideas from real people. Not everyone lives near their folks like I do. I can pop over any afternoon and bring a plate of favorite cookies (or better yet, bake them in her oven so that the house smells delicious) but if I lived a few states over I'd have to come up with a different idea. Even better, my own two sons, young adults, live nearby so I get to have nice things done by them on a semi-regular basis.

Not all adult children live near their parents, and not everyone has a lovey-dovey relationship with their mother, either. In the real world, we have stepmothers, mothers we've chosen, mothers we've lost—all manner of mothering relationships are valid. So not all of these ideas will appeal to all readers; some are too sweet, some might be too tart and tangy, and some may literally be too childlike for the adult you. But do consider what works best for the recipient . . . maybe a little playfulness will do the trick. We hope that some are just right for you and the person you call "Mom."

Sprinkled throughout you'll find sidebars about the newest happiness research, memory research (because hey, we all need that one!), and senior health. We've also included a great many memory moments from contributors, short pieces that remind us all that our sharpest memories come from random small moments rather than elaborately arranged events. So read on, and we hope you find many new ways to amuse, engage, and delight your mother day in and day out.

"To describe my mother would be to write about a hurricane in its perfect power, or the climbing, falling colors of a rainbow."

~Maya Angelou

Grow Her a Garden

Flowers and plants are traditional presents for moms, but why not take it a step further and start them from seeds? Nothing will remind a mother how cute you were in kindergarten than the sight of you, now an adult, offering up a cardboard egg tray filled with potting soil and tiny seedlings. This is a project you can start almost any time of the year; you don't have to wait for spring or summer.

If you want to move beyond the egg tray and invest in a cell tray for starting seeds, you can find them at any garden store. To get started you will want to moisten your soil just enough to hold together in your hand. If it is too wet the seeds might rot. Fill your tray with soil and gently tamp down the soil, leaving about a half inch on top. Now you are ready to add seeds, and then add soil to cover the tops.

"I put mine in flats on top of the refrigerator, or over a heat duct," says organic grower Nina Foster of Trillium Finch. "Heat is great in helping germination. Keep the soil moist—I use a spray bottle. Once the plants have sprouted I put them over by a window for natural light, but remember to rotate every so often as the seedlings will lean towards the light." Once the baby plants start to emerge you have a nice little green gift to take to your mother and plant in her garden.

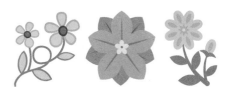

"Victory garden." Ever heard the term? These were home gardens to produce fruits, vegetables, and herbs during World War II. Your mother might have heard the term if she grew up in the post war years. If your mother doesn't already have a veggie garden growing now, it is high time she started (with your help, of course). Fresh vegetables and fruits from our own gardens are packed with the nutrition we all need.

Magical Mom Moments

Our mail was delivered into the aluminum rural-style mailbox which my dad mounted on a stand strategically placed near the front porch of our home. There were times when the stacks of mail astonished me, especially at Christmas.

When the new family room added space to our 1950s-style home, Dad built wooden valances over the sliding doors and windows. When the mail arrived with the many holiday cards, Mom placed them on top of the valances. With amazement, I counted nearly 100 cards. It wasn't just the holidays but all year long. "Mom," I asked, "who are they from?" She got out her address book and showed me, talking me through treasured family and friends. As I grew up, it helped me understand Dad's side of our family from Mom's side of the family. They both came from large families and as a young girl, I thought of them as one big family.

Mom, a very organized woman, updated births, marriages, moves. She changed names, added notes and anniversary dates. A few entries noted illness.

My mom and I were very close. We shared many days together. Her address book had a permanent place on the table next to her chair. It wasn't unusual for me to walk into

6

her home and find her looking through her address book or at least finding that she was holding it. She often updated me about her friends, those who were sick, who passed away. Our conversations began with current letters from family and friends. She was very connected. During her eighty-five years she probably sent thousands of cards and letters full of heartfelt communications to those dear to her.

Her address book was always full. Yes, time had taken some, but many remained. When I shared her passing with my cousins, aunts and uncles, and her dearest friends, the cards poured in with little stories and tidbits about Mom. They included new and fresh accounts full of love honoring a woman who was their lifelong friend. It was a gift she passed on to me.

We keep address books on our phones in today's world, but nothing compares to the handwritten entries marked with comments about those we hold close.

—Claire Manon

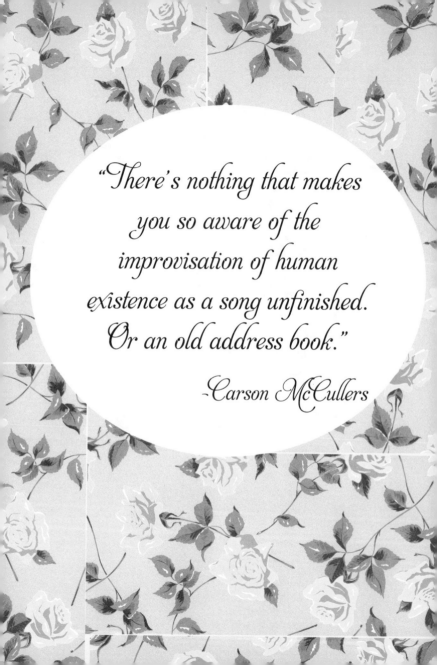

"There's nothing that makes you so aware of the improvisation of human existence as a song unfinished. Or an old address book."

-Carson McCullers

Honor Flights for
Moms Who Served

Did your mother serve in the military? If so, she may well qualify for one of the Honor Flights that leave from all over the country and head to our nation's capital. Founded in 2005, the Honor Flight Network has so far taken over two hundred thousand vets to Washington, DC, to visit the National World War II Memorial.

Originally focused on vets of World War II, they are now also honoring those who served in the Korean and Vietnam Wars Wayne Heple, a veteran of the Korean War, recently took part in a flight that included several women vets. He shared, "There was an entire moving presentation to honor one of the women in our group, Geraldine Bande, a World War II veteran. Photos and speeches, it was wonderful. And it was a total surprise to her, her reaction was neat to watch."

You can find out more information about the organization and their trips at Honorflight.org

Bake Off!

Are you and your mother dedicated bakers? Knocking out the cookies, cakes, and pies week after week for friends and family? Well, then why not up the stakes and enter a baking contest? We'll leave it up to you to decide whether to compete against each other in the same category or perhaps work together on a joint project. There are baking contests everywhere; chances are your state or county fair runs one in the summertime. You can find a contest near you at contestcook.com. The famous King Arthur Flour company also sponsors baking contests at many fairs and festivals like the North Carolina Blueberry Festival or the Adams Agricultural Fair in Massachusetts. You will need to use their product of course, and include proof of purchase along with your baked entry. Check out kingarthurflour.com to find one near you.

Perhaps you'd like to develop an original recipe with your mother to enter into contests? As long as neither of you is a food professional, you could develop a recipe and enter the biannual Pillsbury Bake-Off contest with a $50,000 first prize. Develop an original recipe of no more than eight ingredients (one of which must be an eligible Pillsbury product) and you and your mother could be on your way. Check Pillsbury.com to see when the next contest is being held.

Another contest that might be a good project with your mother is the *Taste of Home* Vintage Recipes from Mom and Grandma Recipe Contest. Maybe there is an award-winning recipe lurking in your family cupboards . . . you never know until you try! For info visit tasteofhome.com

Magical Mom Moments

All her life my Mother was plagued by the reputation of being "serious," but although that title was wished on her, and was based in a deep truth, it was hardly the whole picture. Her given name was "Erna," the diminutive of "Earnest," and growing up, because she was serious and disciplined and dutiful, she was plagued by the sobriquet, "She is so *earnest*." However, this was only part of the picture as I, and my father before me, knew only too well.

I remember one time in Hamburg, we rode the streetcar downtown to the elegant shopping district near the Alster Chausé. Of course, even after more than fifty years away, Hamburg was still Mother's hometown, and though she had grown up in a working-class district, in a Hamburg that no longer even existed, she truly "owned" the City. I remember, we looked for an elusive recording by the great Viennese tenor Richard Taüber, and Mother indulged me by going into a number of terribly elegant antique shops.

At the end of our outing, we went into Moüvenpik, the very "smart" Hamburg *Conditorei*, where we drank incredible coffee, accompanied by slices of the most heavenly *Pflaumen Küchen* with big dollops of *Schlagsahne*. It was an overcast

October day, at the onset of a cold, grey Northern European winter, but Mother and I were warm and happy (both wearing the life-saving silk long-underwear Mother had ordered for our trip), the two of us having a deliciously companionable moment together. Mother's mother had always baked plum tart for her own October birthday (it's made with Schewetchen, a type of plum that only comes onto the market in fall), so there was an element of great nostalgia inherent in the moment . . .

Anyway, we practically licked our plates clean. And then I looked at Monica (Monica was the name she had chosen in place of Erna when she was naturalized an American citizen), and she looked at me—and with a delighted "Little Lulu" gleam in her eye (one my dear father would have recognized instantly) she said, "Let's have *another* one!"

So, we did! (And more Mocca-Java, of *course*!)

—Franklin John Kakies

Try New Tastes

Restaurant choices and cuisine styles seem to increase daily. Chances are you and your mother both already have a favorite type of food, but why not decide to go out and try something totally new together? You may be well-versed in Chinese and Japanese, but have you sampled Tibetan food? Raw food? Ethiopian? Just give it a try, and you might discover a new favorite cuisine together. Scientists tell us that new experiences create new pathways in our brains—what better way to create a new pathway than with an interesting dinner?

Stimulating your taste cortex (actually called the gustatory cortex) by trying new types of foods is a great way to promote brain health. Basic lifestyle choices can create new growth in brain cells, so get out there and try something new—new foods, new places, new ideas—with your mother as often as you can; you both will benefit.

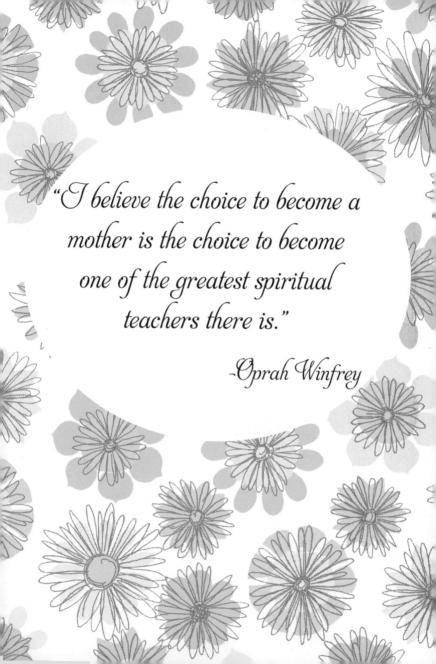

"I believe the choice to become a mother is the choice to become one of the greatest spiritual teachers there is."

-Oprah Winfrey

Magical Mom Moments

One morning in 1990, I woke and sat up on the edge of the bed. A very clear voice inside me said, "It's a boy." I was forty-one and thrilled to be pregnant, and as it turned out, this was to be our only child. At night I lay on the bed with my husband, talking and laughing, wondering how it felt to our baby boy to be bounced around in my heaving belly. We were happy, so I was sure it could only be good for him. Nevertheless, my water broke twenty-four weeks into my pregnancy. At week thirty-one, my husband and I went to the hospital for a checkup, but at 4:30 that Monday afternoon our son was delivered by C-section. We named him Eric Jacob. He was nine weeks premature and weighed 3 pounds, 1.5 ounces.

I'm not sure why, but I had great confidence in him and believed that he would be fine because he was so loved and not easily ruffled. Unlike most babies, he didn't lose any weight after he was born, and I thought, "Yes, he knows what to do . . . just take it easy and grow."

On the hospital ward for "preemies," Eric lived in an incubator for a while, then moved into a tiny, open air bed. He was poked with needles until the heels of his feet looked scarred.

Every day I held him and kissed him, cooed, and spoke to him. Soon he was strong enough to nurse, an immense pleasure for me. When he reached 4.5 pounds, we were allowed to bring him home.

As Eric grew, he said and did funny things, and I wrote them down. I also started a rhyming poem when he was small, and on each of his birthdays I read it to him, having added one or two stanzas about his life during the previous year. I still love reading all the funny things he said, but sometimes he was more serious. One evening when he was three, we looked out his bedroom window together, across the watery rice patties to the lights of Sacramento. He said quietly, "Look at the night, how dark and beautiful." My heart leaped.

—Wendy Watson

Drive-In Movies

Remember how special it was in your childhood to have the family pile into a station wagon and head out for an evening at the drive-in movies? Or maybe your family preferred to cozy up in the living room with fresh popcorn . . . now is the time to relive those moments in a nostalgic bubble, because the bubble is fading fast!

The very first drive-in movie theater opened on June 6, 1933, in Camden, New Jersey. The slogan was "The whole family is welcome, regardless of how noisy the children are." They soon became a national phenomenon. At the peak there were four thousand around the country, but that has now dwindled to just over three hundred. Is there still one near you? You can find out at driveinmovie.com.

So pack up some candy and popcorn, throw some blankets in the car, and head out for a fun evening. Maybe you can even round up your siblings!

Deep Cleaning

Is there an RV at your mother's house? Why not treat her to a surprise deep cleaning of her traveling home? This is a gift idea that could be a way for the whole family to do something special for your mother. Even small children can dust (perhaps not that well, but heck, give them a rag anyway).

If your family rents a recreational vehicle for vacations you don't need to worry about this (part of the joys of non-ownership), but many RV owners have their rigs sitting in the driveway for months on end between use, so they always need a good dusting before heading out on to the open road.

"What little tricks did mom teach you?" asks Ingrid Lundquist. "Using newspaper to clean windows, vinegar and water to clean glass, or using baking soda to unclog the drains?" So, as long as there is family cleaning going on, why not compile a little book of your mother's (and her mother's) cleaning ideas?

Magical Mom Moments

American Gothic plus three children: my mother and her brother stand between their seated parents, baby on their father's lap, in front of the white Illinois farmhouse our family had already had for three generations as the Depression began. This is the earliest photograph I have of my mother, and it will begin the memory book I am putting together for her now. At ninety-six, she has just moved into a memory care wing. Perhaps these pictures with captions in large type will spark memories, perhaps not. But the book will help the staff as they help her with daily activities. The picture bingo game they play has a card with a suitcase on it, so it can lead to questions like: "Marjorie, you did lots of traveling, didn't you? I see you went on a safari in Africa once." "You don't like your dinner? I'll bet you did a better job of planning meals as a dietician. Where did you go to college again? The first one in your family, weren't you?" "I know you love sitting here, reading and looking out at the birds and pine trees. You did a lot of reading at your cabin in Montana, didn't you?"

As I sort through the photos, I am in awe of the life she led and the challenges she conquered. Raised on a farm with no electricity or indoor plumbing, she sold eggs for the only cash she had in the Depression. She learned what she could

in a one-room schoolhouse and earned a full scholarship to university. I wonder, did the young man in uniform with her at a college dance survive the war? I see my father's medical school graduation, a small, frugal wedding, and four moves in ten years as three children came along. A time of blossoming followed, with a family cabin, graduations, weddings, grandchildren, and travels all over the world. Jeep trips and hiking filled their retirement in Sedona. But gradually her loved ones have disappeared from the photos—parents, brothers, husband, a daughter. Soon, she too will be gone, but the book I make for her now will keep her memories for all of us.

—Kathryn Canan

Memoirs about Moms and Mothering

Do the rich and famous have easier lives and better relationships than more ordinary folks like us? No. Here are several memoirs that give a glimpse into the joys and struggles of famous children, and will perhaps remind your mother that she is blessed to have you in her life.

Mom & Me & Mom

By Maya Angelou

In the final volume in her series of autobiographies, Angelou reveals how she went from calling her mother "Lady" in her earlier life, to finally calling her "Mom." An emotional tale of separation and eventual reunion.

The Rainbow Comes and Goes: A Mother and Son on Life, Love, and Loss

By Gloria Vanderbilt and Anderson Cooper

The late Gloria Vanderbilt and her son, television journalist Anderson Cooper, worked together on a book that showcases their personally revealing correspondence on a variety of topics.

Then Again

By Diane Keaton

Diane Keaton's mother was named Dorothy Hall, and she is every bit as interesting as her actress daughter. Using her mother's copious personal journals for material, Diane Keaton unspools her family story.

Elsewhere: A Memoir

By Richard Russo

Novelist Richard Russo reveals his mother's restlessness with small town life, and how she followed him across the country when he went away to college.

Bettyville: A Memoir

By George Hodgman

The late George Hodgman left his grown-up and sophisticated life in New York to return home to Missouri and become the caretaker for his ailing mother.

Is it time to help your own mother write her memoir? You can give her a copy of *Mom's Journal: A Keepsake of What I Want You to Know About Me and My Life,* with fill-in-the-blank areas to answer questions that will help her memories flow easily onto the page.

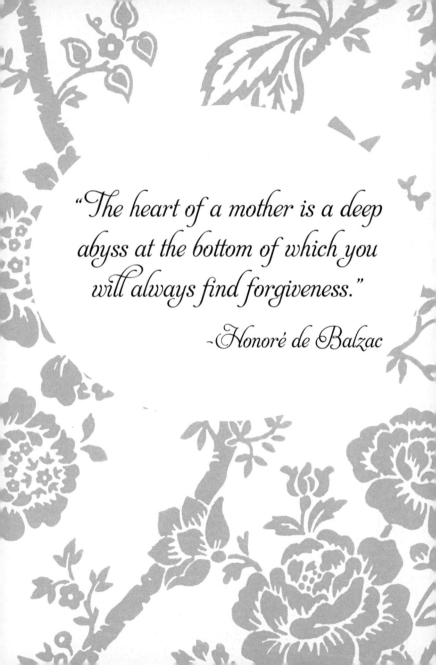

"The heart of a mother is a deep abyss at the bottom of which you will always find forgiveness."

-Honoré de Balzac

Help with Her Hang Ups

Does your mother have a selection of framed photos and artwork leaning against a wall in a dusty corner? Might be time to ask if you can help her hang them up. We will all get a tad stiff in the shoulders eventually, and climbing up on a ladder isn't the most secure feeling for women of a certain age. Chances are she will welcome your assistance, and it will give her a chance to stand back and say, "No, wait . . . just a little to the right. Oh, okay, down an inch or so and that should be fine. Actually, now that I look at it . . ."

Magical Mom Moments

I was lucky to be an only child and loved the doting. My parents divorced before I was twelve. Mom was concerned that I wouldn't have the male influence necessary to develop into a moral and ethical young man, so she volunteered as Cub Scout Leader. She followed the programs, leading, in those days, other young boys following the outdoor skills, educational programs, and activities. I was so proud of her. She shared her love of the outdoors by taking me to most of the National Parks. I remember great trips full of laughter and just plain silliness.

The Boy Scouts of America were considered a progressive movement during the mid-twentieth century. With her leadership and guidance I became an Eagle Scout, one of over 2.5 million youth. That accomplishment at a young age has significantly helped me in my life. Later, I enlisted in the Army, followed by a career in law enforcement.

When my mother showed signs of dementia, my wife and I moved her into our home where she lived until it became dangerous for her and she required more care than we could safely provide. She lived close by. As she waned, she knew who I was. Her eyes lit up with that sparkle I always knew.

Her final request of me was to scatter her ashes in the mountains, places where we shared beautiful days and wonderful conversations. And, we still can.

—Ken MacHold

Microsoft founder and philanthropist Bill Gates has been awarded the Silver Buffalo, the highest Boy Scout honor in the US, for his services to youth. As both a cub and scout, Mr. Gates achieved the rank of Life Scout. Many women have been the behind-the-scenes (or an out front) motivator for scouts trying to attain the Eagle Scout rank. "More than one-third of Scout volunteers are women," according to scouting.org. Was your mother one of them?

Beautifully Arranged

Fresh flowers in the house are always a welcome sight. Even better if they are beautifully arranged. Flower arranging doesn't need to be intimidating—keep it seasonal and simple but make sure to vary the heights and textures and colors and put it all in a pretty vessel of some sort. Be sure to strip away the leaves that are on the bottom of the stem (they will rot underwater and hasten the demise of your pretty arrangement) and make a fresh cut on the bottom, always at an angle to help the flower absorb water. If you can't come up with an arrangement that works with what you have on hand, you can always check out a hundred or so photos on Pinterest for inspiration. No need to worry about making it look professional; even plain flowers in a vase will warm your mother's heart.

Are you using locally grown flowers in your arrangements? You are if they came from your own backyard, of course, but otherwise it is hard to tell. Just like the movement towards local, organic food, the flower world is also organizing around the idea that local flowers are best. Take your mother out to the local farmers market and choose fresh flowers together or visit a local flower farm. Slowflowers.com is a great source of information on where to find growers near you.

"My favorite floral memory is from when I was a little girl growing up in rural Vermont," says flower farmer Nina Foster. "I would entertain myself out in the meadows and hedgerows. Even back then I was foraging and harvesting lots of wild treasures like goldenrod, daisies, bittersweet, Queen Anne's lace. I would make elaborate wreaths and bouquets, as elaborate as a small child can make, anyway. I would arrive home with all my offerings for my mom, armloads some days. She always smiled and told me how beautiful they were and thanked me so much for bringing them to her . . . she encouraged me, day after day. We had enough wild florals for the whole village! She was always my biggest supporter, right from the beginning."

"Only mothers can think of the future, because they give birth to it in their children."

-Maxim Gorky

Pie Day

Who doesn't love pie? Freshly baked out of the oven, or a frothy whipped cream pie concoction? Pie has many fans; maybe you and your mother are among them. If so, scoop your mother up some afternoon and go for a pie run. Is there a famed pie palace in your town? Many areas have them, from Sweet Delights in Miami, Florida, to the Pie Snob in Phoenix, Arizona, and up to the Calico Cupboard in La Conner, Washington. You could plan an entire vacation around hunting for good pie if you were so inclined. In which case you'd both better bring along an extra, slightly larger, set of clothes.

National Pie Day is January 23 (not to be confused with National Pi Day, on March 14), so that might be a great time to plan your pie-seeking adventures. If you can't wait that long, then how about tomorrow? A slice of pie is good anytime!

Where do these "National" days come from, anyway? They often start with folks just like you declaring a day to honor something they love. A nuclear engineer from Colorado, Charlie Papazian, was the first to declare his own birthday as National Pie Day and it was soon taken up and promoted by the American Pie Council.

Magical Mom Moments

In the early 2000s video game *Duck Dodgers*, Daffy ventures to distant planets to save the earth, risking life and feathers. When the lasers and bombs get the best of him, he utters one word: "Mother," and sinks to a pile of ashes.

That one word can mean so much. In this case, it is a sign that he has had enough of superhero theatrics and needs a bit of saving himself. In my years as a mom, it has been used to express emotions that could not otherwise have been said.

That first "ma-ma," much anticipated and tentatively uttered, was a sign that we both were coming to terms with the fact that we were not one person, but two bodies sharing one heart. When my daughter was two and venturing out to the playground the first time, when she called "Mommy" from the sandbox, she really just wanted to know I was there. And I let her know with a hand on the back. No other words were needed for her to return to throwing plastic toys in the air.

When my son was twelve and busy in the garage with his best friend—duct-taping themselves to a chair on a skate-board—when I asked if that was really a good idea, "Mom," was the encapsulation of all the excitement, fear, and

independence he couldn't articulate. I interpreted it as, "Please tell me not to do this thing so I can blame you."

When at thirty, my daughter called me and asked hypothetically, for a friend, "Mother, what is the best way to get red wine out of a white sofa?" we all knew what that meant.

When my mother was lying in a hospital bed after the doctors had "done all they could," and I placed my forehead on her head with just the lightest dusting of gray hairs left, and uttered that word, it was a stand-in for all the things I couldn't say. All the times I couldn't be there. All the things I wish I could have taken back. All the things I wish I could have done for her. Thanks for all the things she did for me. It was all of that and more.

—JT Long

A Holiday of One's Own

The real history of Mother's Day is touching—in 1868 a woman named Ann Jarvis created a "Mother's Friendship Day" as a post–Civil War effort. After her efforts, her own daughter Anna Reeves Jarvis took it a step further and got it officially established early in the twentieth century.

So, if you were to create a holiday for your mother, what would it be? Why not declare a different day during the year to be her own special day, fashioned around her interests and the things she cares about. Does she like to garden? You can celebrate her favorite flower. National Rose month is in June (and National Rosé day is June 8, in case she likes to drink a glass on occasion). You can also borrow one of the "days" that already exist, like National Donut Day or National Chocolate Chip Cookie Day. Once you decide on a theme you can really go all out—designing the themed party décor, creating a special menu, making a big poster celebrating her.

"If I were going to create a yearly holiday for my own mother, Mary Alice, I'd call it National Shine Your Silver and Copper Day, as that would be a great way to put a smile on her face and enshrine something she personally cares about—gleaming things in the kitchen. Choose an idea close to your mother's heart."

—Gin Sander

"By the time you realize your mother was right, you have a daughter who thinks that you are wrong."

-Sada Malhotra

Tour the Town

Does your mother still live in the town she grew up in? If not, is it nearby and close enough for a day trip? Why not take her on a tour of her own town? Drive around and ask her to tell you stories about specific moments in her life. "Tell me about the department store that used to be on this corner . . . isn't that where you bought your wedding dress?"

Or perhaps you can take her on a tour of your childhood haunts, the grammar school, your best friend's house, your after-school spot. Maybe it is time to finally confess what you were up to on those long afternoons? After all, it's not like she can ground you anymore!

Is she visiting you in your town? Why not round up your mother and check out what's new? Brew pubs? They spring up like weeds! Trendy ice cream shops? You'll need to visit them all! Artist and makers' spaces? What could be hipper?

You've no doubt heard of a "staycation"—taking a vacation by staying in your own house or town. Maybe your mother needs a staycation too. Think up ways that you can make her house feel like a hotel for a few days, maybe with meal service, or a visit from a mobile massage therapist? Have fun thinking of ideas that would make her smile.

Creative Cards

The retail world is full of greeting cards; every grocery store has a huge aisle devoted to cards for every occasion. And it can be a fun task to stand in front of the rack and open a few dozen to find something that does the trick. But you know what is a welcome treat anytime, for any occasion or no reason at all? A handmade card.

Not much is required to make a greeting card; just some thick card stock and a colored pen or two. Fold the paper in half and get to work. You can easily create a collaged card by cutting out photos or images from magazines to glue in your card. Glitter is always a nice touch, but make sure it is well glued to the paper as no one wants to spend the afternoon vacuuming up after they open a greeting card.

Side by Side Pedicures

A pedicure is a most enjoyable indulgence, isn't it? To be perched up on what we can pretend is a throne, while a lovely person pampers our feet! Chances are your mother loves the experience too. So why not do side by side pedis? If you do it once, you might find that you have to schedule it more often—it is a habit that is hard to break.

With older moms, this also has a practical side. As we age (and we will get there too someday, knock on wood), our ability to bend over and clip our own toenails becomes hard to maintain. Balance and flexibility do fade with the years. Having a regular pedicure with your mother is a tactful way of helping her deal with that situation without having to 'fess up that she is having trouble with the task.

A quick caveat on pedicures for much older women—their skin becomes thin and an ordinary pedicure might well be too rough. Sometimes a visit to a podiatrist is required; check with your mother's doctor if you aren't sure.

Magical Mom Moments

After I was born, my grandparents took a trip to Europe. They purchased a painting of a Madonna and Child and gave it to my mother, saying that the baby in the painting looked just like me. Recently, my Mom handed the painting down to me, repeating the oft-told story of my resemblance to the Baby Jesus in this work of art.

Later I discovered that this particular painting is the symbol of the Gabriel Project of the Catholic Church. They use this image to encourage pregnant women who are considering abortion to keep their babies.

As I prepared to teach an Art History class in Florence, Italy, I thought about that Madonna and Child and the many others that my grandmother had collected in her travels. I own several of her prized pieces. I started to reflect on the abundance of Madonna and Child images in the Renaissance. So many of these are so beautiful in their own way. I decided it would be a great exercise for the students to select their favorite out of all we saw.

I find these images particularly poignant as I tie them to what is often the happiest time in a mother's life—when the child is young, under the mother's protection, and kept from harm. As a child grows older, the mother cannot constantly control the child's environment and safety.

I also think of these joy-filled images in contrast to the pathos of Michelangelo's Pieta, when the Virgin mourns her dead son, holding him in her lap as if he were still a child. Being a mother can bring the highest point of happiness and the greatest point of agony and pain.

—Dr. Cary C. Rote

"Mothers are all
slightly insane."

-J.D. Salinger, from
The Catcher in the Rye

Bird Count

Every year the Audubon Society organizes volunteer bird counts, and thousands of bird lovers lend a hand. If your mother has an interest in bird watching (or maybe hasn't ever tried) this is a great thing you two can do together. The Great Backyard Bird Count, or the GBBC as it is known to participants, takes place over a four-day span every February. And it is just what it sounds like—you count the birds in your own backyard. There is also a photo contest element where you can enter the pictures you've taken of the birds you've spotted. Find out the information at gbbc.birdcount.org

Luxurious Sleep Station

Ready to splurge on a little gift for your mother? It doesn't need to be a pair of diamond studs; for far less you can give her a luxurious set of sheets. Really good quality sheets are the sort of thing we seldom think of as having fit potential, but they truly are a fabulous and indulgent gift. Gifting some luxurious sheets to your mother is a great way for her to feel special if she is not living close to you. Every night she can slip between her new high thread count cotton sheets and be reminded of your thoughtfulness. Or that is the goal, anyway. . . .

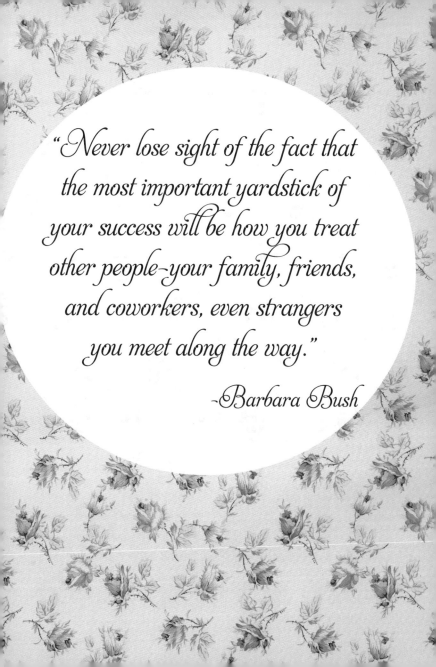

"Never lose sight of the fact that the most important yardstick of your success will be how you treat other people—your family, friends, and coworkers, even strangers you meet along the way."

-Barbara Bush

Magical Mom Moments

The word "Mom" is synonymous with baking and childhood memories of waking to the smell of cinnamon rolls and the kids coming over after school because Mom perfectly timed the cookies so they were cooled just enough not to burn the roof of our mouths. The aroma at dinner time was that of fresh baked rolls or the sweetness of a dessert made from scratch.

Like in the bathroom, which had a light dusting of what I thought of as Mother's Day talcum powder after Mom's morning shower (I gave her a can every year, or maybe my father did), there were always fine grains of flour that seemed to be suspended in air above the kitchen appliances. Mom had a baking drawer that held bags of flour, different kinds of sugar, sifters, measuring cups, a rolling pin, and a clean white flour sack dish towel to use if something needed to be covered while it cooled. She'd pull out the recipe ingredients, measure them, mix it all up, return everything to their assigned place in the drawer, and pop the treat in the oven. While the treat was baking, it was not unusual for her to then pull the supplies out again and mix up a batch of something different.

Mom had sets of measuring cups for both dry and liquid ingredients. She never washed the dry measuring cups, explaining that there was no possible way to contain all the particles of flour so there would always be rogue flour in the baking drawer. "Just knock the extra flour out of the cup when you're done and it's ready to use again," she said. "If you get it wet and then need to use it right away, you could end up with wheat paste stuck in the cup."

I bake a lot because I'm comforted by the memory of Mom in the kitchen. I have a deep drawer with sugar, flour, yeast, salt, baking powder, and baking soda, and I never wash my dry measuring cups. The flour dust is as much a part of the memory as making the house smell like home.

—Ingrid Lundquist

Move Outdoors

What we used to call "taking a walk in the park," or maybe "hiking," is now sometimes referred to as "forest bathing." If nothing else, tell your mother that going outside is now called "forest bathing," and we promise she will get a good laugh out of it.

No doubt you are already aware of the tremendous health benefits involved in simply being outdoors—lower blood pressure, reduced depression, and reduced anxiety to name just a few. We take it for granted though, and forget to make an effort to step outside and take our mothers with us.

The Japanese have embraced the idea of forest bathing as an antidote to their stressful city life. According to *Afar* magazine, in 2018 there were almost 5 million people walking the healing forest trails and 1,200 certified forest bathing guides to help them along the way.

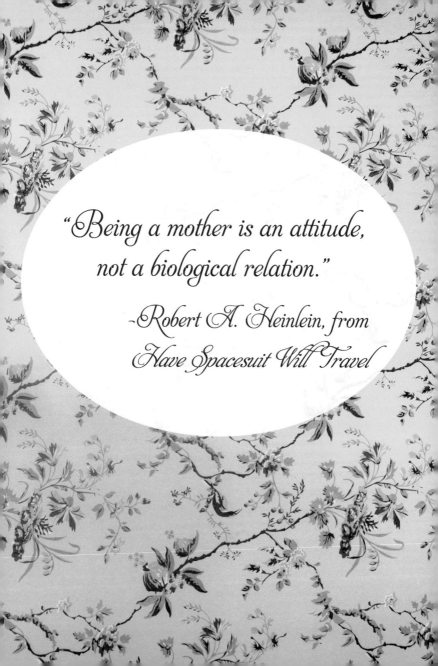

"Being a mother is an attitude, not a biological relation."

-Robert A. Heinlein, from *Have Spacesuit Will Travel*

Create a Small Book Club

Do you and your mother like to read the same kind of books? If so, why not form your own two-person book club? And if you don't read the same kind of books, what better reason to form your own two-person book club and get to know each other's interests?

Book clubs have been popular for several decades and are still going strong. Reese Witherspoon is the latest celeb to pick up the book club idea, and you can find her "Reese's Book Club x Hello Sunshine" on Instagram or Facebook and check out her most recent pick. Among the books she has fallen for are *This is the Story of a Happy Marriage*, by Ann Patchett, and *Where the Crawdads Sing*, by Delia Owens.

Talking about something in a book can sometimes be a safer way of talking about something in your own lives, a way to tackle sensitive family topics without confrontation. Or maybe just a way to share a laugh together. Will Schwalbe created a book club for two with his own mother after she received a dire diagnosis. He wrote a book about it after she passed away. *The End of Your Life Book Club* chronicles their experience and might be a good source of books for you to start off reading and discussing with your own mother.

My own mother just finished reading *These Truths: A History of the United States*, by Jill Lepore. "So," I asked her, "what was the most surprising thing you learned?" "That there is so much of it," she said. End of conversation.

—Gin Sander

Magical Mom Moments

My eight-year-old heart and head had been struggling for a couple years to understand why my loving mama left us. Suicide was something I needed so badly to understand in order to go on living. But I couldn't. All I knew was I needed her and she was not there and I would never see her again.

My dad remarried a few years later. Driving to our new mom's home from the church, my dad announced that we were now a family. I hopefully responded, "Does that mean we get to call her 'Mom'?" But she answered, "No, I'm still Dorothy to you." All hope left my soul as I realized as long as he was married to this woman I would not ever have another mother. I was devastated, but as the years of emotional and physical abuse followed, I never gave up. At some point I started calling her Mom anyway.

At age sixteen, I was pregnant and moved in with the boy's family. When I would come to visit my dad he would always walk me out to the driveway, Dorothy right behind him to make sure he didn't give me money or anything she didn't want me to have, then I'd hug Dad goodbye. One day I had the urge to hug her in spite of her anger. So, I quickly leaned in to hug her and she pushed me away. Each visit I would

make a game of it and try to catch her off guard so I could get in there faster than her and hug her. But, she would always push me away. Each visit as I walked to the end of the driveway I would look back and say, "I love you, Mom."

After several attempts over the years, one day when I went in for the hug she dropped her head on my shoulder and started crying. She sobbed into my ear, "I love you." She told me she was sorry for treating me so badly and from that day until she died she was truly my "Mom."

—Donnella Fradkin

Back to School

After book club for two, why not take it a step further and enroll in a class together? Remember, change keeps us young. So is it time to brush up on your French or renew your interest in classic literature? Perhaps your mother would like to join you.

Taking a class together will give you fresh topics to discuss (maybe you both will crush on the professor). And this is something that would work if you and your mother live in different towns or parts of the country. Choose a topic that interests you both, and then try to find local classes near you that are offered at the same time. You might not be sitting next to each other in class, but you are having a parallel experience and can still discuss what you are learning and how you feel about the new information.

"It was a shared excitement," Ingrid Lundquist says about taking college classes at the same time as her mother Jessamine. "We went together, but we went our own way to our classes—hers was on a trendy thing at the time, 'psychocybernectics,' and mine was biology. Then when we got back into the car we had much to discuss about what happened in our classes. It was only one summer but I remember it well."

Clean Out That Garage

You don't want to clean your own garage; no one really wants to tackle that task. So the chances are the garage (or perhaps attic, or basement) at your folks' house could use some help at this point too. We predict your mother will be thrilled—who turns down a free cleaning?

Make sure to have her somewhere nearby when you are tackling this task as you will need her okay on what to toss. A sweet and loving gesture could easily turn ugly if you accidently toss a meaningful memento. And be sure to engage her in conversation as you clean and sort—asking "Mom, where did this come from?" for a few hours on a Saturday afternoon could lead to you learning all manner of new info about your family history.

You can also have fun with the "spark joy" idea popularized by Marie Kondo, the Japanese organizing consultant who wrote the bestselling *The Life-Changing Magic of Tidying Up*. Ask your mother about the things you are finding in the garage or attic, "Does this spark joy?" If not, Kondo says it must go.

The average American home has about 300,000 individual items. From tubes of toothpaste and bars of soap to beds and lamps and couches, that is a pretty overwhelming fact to wrap your head around.

"If at first you don't succeed, try doing it the way your mom told you to in the beginning."

-Unknown

Home and Garden Tours

Does your mother enjoy the many home decorating or garden design shows on cable television? You can treat her to a live walk-through experience of houses and gardens decorated to the nth degree. From coast to coast, every spring a new crop of Decorator Showcases emerge—from the famous San Francisco Decorator Showcase in April to the Kips Bay Decorator Showcase in May and many places in between—and you can tour these gorgeous mansions to your heart's delight. A source of non-profit fundraising for schools and hospitals, decorators and designers donate their talents every year to produce amazing eye candy and, dare we say it, "house porn." Holiday-themed showcases crop up in the winter, and summer brings scores of garden tours. This is your chance to see over-the-top decorating ideas that you might end up copying in your own home. Or it might just be an afternoon of giggling with your mother at the wild ideas on display. Either way, an afternoon to remember.

Magical Mom Moments

I originally wrote this poem in first person and transposed it over a photo of my mother and me, as a gift for Mom's 90th birthday. Mom kept the framed gift next to her chair so she would never forget—not only that *she* was loved, but that I knew she loved me too.

Our Mother

*Our Mother Charlotte brought us into this world
And she loved us.*

She loved us gently
she loved us rough

Her heart grew for us
 her heart broke for us

She cheered for us
she cried for us

She laughed with us
she yelled at us

She trusted us
she worried for our souls

She ignored us
she listened to us

She taught us
she learned from us

She scolded us
she admired us

She was always, always, there for us

Our mother Charlotte
brought us into this world
and she loved us

Mom made her transition three weeks before her 92nd birthday and my siblings and I felt this poem was a sweet eulogy, expressing all the ways she loved us, so I changed the pronoun to include her eight children gathered to give her a loving farewell.

—Rose Ann Goodwin

Assemble This (If You Dare)

One of the most useful things we can do for our parents (and soon enough our own children will have to do for us!) is to help them navigate the tech and electronic world. If your mom is young enough that you haven't yet gotten a call asking for your help to increase the type size on her Kindle, or help her upgrade her computer, you will. And the same goes for the rest of our do-it-yourself world in which we pump our own gas, self-check at the grocery store, and put together our own bookshelves from Ikea. Why not get ahead of the game and make it a point to ask often if there is anything your mother needs assembled? Or perhaps disassembled!

If you have children yourself, this is a task that you can strong-arm them into helping with. Young eyesight and small hands are essential tools for assembling things, and young brains are (sadly) always better at any electronic device.

Fund Together

In the mood for a little philanthropy? Why not sit down and discuss funding a cause that you both care about? Big sums are not required—even $25 is a welcome addition to any organization's bottom line. Sharing a cup of coffee while talking about various organizations and causes is another way to learn more about each other. You might be surprised to learn your mother's thoughts on the big issues that challenge our world nowadays, and she might be surprised to learn your feelings on issues that are closer to home. Giving together, and then seeing your names linked on the contributor page of your chosen organization, is a warm and wonderful feeling. You are helping a cause you both care about, and you are joining forces to make that happen.

You might be interested in the "giving circle" movement. Although there are many big dollar family foundations, you too can play in that league by forming your own family giving circle. Pam Giarrizzo helped form a giving circle with like-minded friends in California and says, "The giving circle I'm involved with chooses a different local organization to help each month." Simply agree on who you will help, and then all send your individual checks in one envelope.

"I want my children to have all the things I couldn't afford. Then, I want to move in with them."

-Phyllis Diller

Game Night

Just like going to the drive-in movies is a hefty dose of childhood nostalgia (or a chance to create the childhood you never had), so too is staging a game night with your parents. Think back on your own childhood. Were you an avid Candyland player? Or perhaps devoted to Monopoly? Those of us with childhoods that took place in the early days of computer games might well have been SimCity fans.

There is a new golden age of board games emerging, and new games are being released all the time. The extremely popular (and extremely crude) Cards Against Humanity might not be the right choice for you to suggest to your mother, but what about hauling out the old Scrabble board for an after-dinner game? Ask your mother if she has any warm memories of family game nights that you can try to recreate.

Magical Mom Moments

My mom, blessed be her memory, traveled via novels borrowed from the library, and she passed that love of literary traveling onto me.

When I was a homebound seventh grader spotted with measles, she trudged to the local library and searched the shelves for a cure to the boredom caused by my isolation. In that stack of books she set in my room was John Steinbeck's *The Grapes of Wrath*. It was a novel, she told me conspiratorially, that my "friend's mother wouldn't let her read."

Oooh. . . . Of course that was the first book I took to bed with me. Salaciously, I turned each page, devouring the words and story hungrily. By the end, even though I'd read an engaging and memorable story, I was disappointed not to discover the reason a mother would not allow her child to read this.

Mom also introduced me to Betty Smith's *A Tree Grows in Brooklyn* and *The Good Earth* by Pearl S. Buck, among others. We shared literary interests until she died. Like the summer she stayed with me when my kids were preschoolers, and I'd gotten my hands on Alice Walker's *The Color Purple*. I'd be reading it, then put it down to take care of laundry or some other task, but when I came back, the book was in her hands and her eyes were stuck inside those pages. Then she'd put it down for some reason or other and I'd snatch it up, not releasing it until I had to. We continued that way until we each finished the book, and finished it all too soon. That's the way good books do us—leaving us hungry for more. My mom both fed and encouraged that worldly hunger.

—Susan Dlugach

The Doctor Will See You (Both) Now

Is your mother getting up there in years? A medical appointment is stressful under the best of circumstances, but the older the patient, the more stressful it becomes. From actually getting there—navigating the car ride, parking lot, elevator, and so on—to the actual time spent with the doctor or nurse practitioner, having a companion makes the ordeal a bit more bearable. A second person listening, adding information, and asking questions during the appointment is invaluable.

If you live nearby, offer to come and pick your mother up. If you live out of town, when making plans to visit ask about upcoming appointments and perhaps you can schedule your visit to coincide. Another way to be involved in her doctor visits is to help her prep the topics she wants to discuss with the doctor during the appointment. A phone conversation the night before will help prompt her to remember all of the various sorts of information she is seeking from the visit or questions she'd like answered.

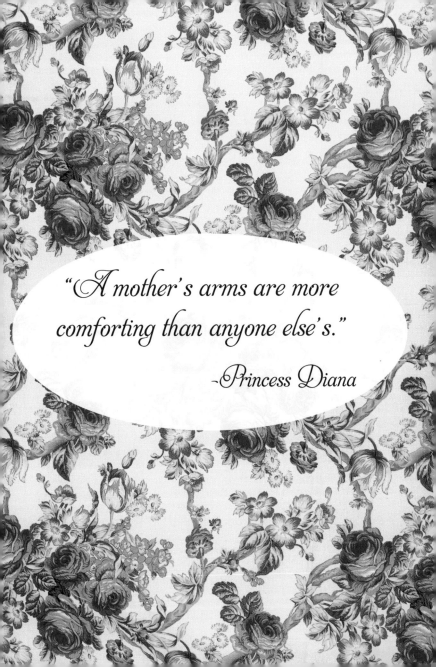

"A mother's arms are more comforting than anyone else's."

-Princess Diana

Magical Mom Moments

Small children have an undeserved reputation as finicky eaters who limit themselves to macaroni and cheese. My two boys turned out to crave French brie and water crackers, freshly picked organic blueberries, and Dungeness crab. After one particularly expensive meal I'd had enough. Waving my hand toward the window, I directed my sons' attention to the beach just outside. "See that, guys? It's called an ocean. Lots of things live in the ocean, including," and here I held up a crab leg to help drive home my point, "crab." Their eyes lit up with a strange fire I'd not seen before. "So, we can catch them and kill them?" Leave it to a small boy to cut to the chase.

I bought a book, always my first step to learning something new. I learned all manner of crab-related facts—including that they love to eat decaying food. When it comes to crab bait, the more putrid the better. But best of all, I learned I can get two young boys to spend endless amounts of time with their mommy, away from their phones and games, in hot pursuit of crab.

Our first boat was a "wet-bottom boat," an inflatable row boat in which your bottom really would be soaked. My sons

wanted to call it *The Sequoia*. Their little girl cousin wanted it to be *The Barbie*. So *The Barbie-Sequoia* was born. We'd load it up with baited crab rings, line, and buoys, and row out off-shore to set our traps.

A large live crab can be a bit intimidating. Those big claws filled with juicy meat can inflict real damage to fingers when still attached to a crab. Martha Stewart doesn't want to know what goes on when I'm wearing those tasteful green leather gardening gloves I got for Mother's Day a few years back. Let's just say I'm not yanking weeds. The satisfaction of preparing a meal that my sons and I have caught on our own has given me many a happy summer moment, and I hope they continue for years.

—Jennifer Sander

Picture Day

L ooking for a touching way to spend an hour or more with your mother? Ask to see an old family photo album and flip through it together, stopping to talk about the various pictures that intrigue you. Even if it is a photo you think you know well, there might be more behind it. Asking open ended questions like "Who was that?" "Why were you all together that day?" "Did this group ever get together again?" might well spark your mother to share a memory from long ago about old friends, shirttail relatives, or long hidden family drama. If you frame your questions in a way to jog old memories you'll be surprised at what you might learn about your own family or your own childhood. Even if the childish you is smack dab in the center of the photo there may well have been things about that day that escaped your young notice.

Technology has changed the way our memories are preserved, but many family photos and films are still preserved in old school methods like printed photos, old slides, or video tapes. The days when we have actual photo albums to peruse together are dwindling, but there are many businesses that will digitize your family photos. Check out the aptly named ScanMyPhotos.com, or see if there is a similar business in your town. Check out the big drugstores near you; they might offer services like this also. Future generations will be glad you did.

Create a Family Cookbook

No doubt you've noticed that it is easier than ever to put together a simple book. And what could be simpler than a family cookbook project? Well, the cookbook part will be simple—the family part is totally up to you.

Several companies operate in this space, and offer templates that you can use to design the pages and upload the recipes that you have managed to convince everyone in your family to share. Createmycookbook.com and Shutterfly.com are good platforms to investigate. Prices for finished cookbooks range from $19.95 for the simplest binding up to $39.95 for hardcover books with a protective slipcover.

Creating a family cookbook could be a fun way to spend time with your mother in person or over the phone, or it could be a secret project you intend to surprise her with on a special occasion.

Magical Mom Moments

Like many women, I'd anticipatedhaving a career, marriage, and children. We expected to have it all. Then, my first marriage ended in divorce. My husband and I had met on a blind date and were inseparable within a couple of weeks, and engaged within months. That's often the case with second marriages. We just celebrated our twenty-eighth anniversary. At thirty-seven, I brought to our marriage one unruly dog and one cat. At forty-two, he brought to our marriage three daughters. He had married in college and divorced when the girls were in the first, second, and third grades.

One of the first things I loved about him was that he was an amazing single father. He told me a friend taught him that that when combing a mass of long hair to get them ready for school, that you didn't start at the top, but at the bottom, working your way through the tangles. Standing up with us at our wedding were his three daughters. The eldest was college bound. The two younger teenagers in high school. By my side, my maid of honor, a girlfriend in what I thought was a beautiful green satin gown she hated but wore nonetheless. My husband had a very large family. My one sister and her family flew from Indiana for the wedding. The guests also included my collection of solid friendships tended over a lifetime, including some of the best girlfriends a woman could ever have. Friendships between women can be as strong as any blood relative. One of mine refers to them as her "chosen family."

I didn't know how to parent. My husband said my success with his girls was because I didn't try to replace their mother. All I could offer them was my love for their father and friendship. I knew a lot about girlfriends. My stepdaughters were in and out of the house while I had grown used to living alone in a quiet, tidy home. I was faced with messy bedrooms, odd boy-friends, large holiday celebrations, graduations, weddings, and the births of six grandchildren. We all had to adjust and there were challenging times. They had to deal with me box-ing up their abandoned stuff and shipping it to them to create a guest room. Other marriages I've known have failed because the children didn't get along with their stepmother. I've told other friends of mine who waited too long to have children, that they may marry into them.

Unexpectedly, I had the family I'd always dreamed of and all it took was friendship. Many people assume I'm the girls' real mother. I used to correct my status as stepmother because I dared not take credit for these three accomplished women. After thirty years, I now refer to them as "our daughters."

—Nancy Weaver Teichert

The Fam Fave

Is there a more welcoming, nostalgic feeling than the one provoked by the smell of freshly baked cookies? Or the aroma of meatloaf almost ready to come out of the oven? A coffee cake cooling on a sideboard? Your family has a favorite baked dish, no doubt, and your mother would love it if you popped it in the oven.

Not only would the dish itself be welcome, but you can also use this as an opportunity to ask about the recipe. Did she learn it from her mother? Grandmother? Next door neighbor? The story behind the recipe might well be even more tantalizing than the food itself! Cathleen Swanson always loved her mother's German Christmas stollen and was surprised to learn the hidden history of the bread. "I remember my excitement at discovering that the holiday bread was made in a tradition even older than Christianity. The cake bread is in the shape of the crescent moon with a slit in it for when the moon gives birth to the sun to start the new year. I felt proud of my mother for keeping the tradition."

"One of the most important relationships we have is the relationship we have with our mothers."

-Iyanla Vanzant

Play Date

Has it been awhile since your mother saw her friends? Life happens, sometimes physical limitations develop, and old habits fade away. So why not arrange a "play date" for her? Get in touch with her old friends and invite her crew out to the movies, or for a girls' lunch, or a group wine tasting. No need to wait for her birthday or other milestone; organize it just because. And if her friends are all around the same age as she is, chances are they will be delighted at the invitation to get together.

Dancing Queen

Your mother had a life before she had you. And she dated, danced, and may have done many of the same things you did when you were in high school. Hard to imagine now, but probably quite true. So why not ask her to dance now? Ask her to teach you the moves she had back in the day.

Whereas earlier generations had complicated dances like the Lindy Hop, dance seems to have gotten a tad more freestyle. But maybe she can teach you how to do the Twist, the Hustle, or the Funky Chicken from the seventies. Preschool teacher Wendy Brooks tried with her children, but, "Really, anything I do—singing along with the car radio, nodding my head to the beat—is mortifying to them." You, on the other hand, are now mature enough to enjoy the experience. Go ahead, ask your mother to dance!

Is she in a wheelchair? You can use hand movements or get her wheelchair to dance. There are many videos on YouTube to give you inspiration and ideas. Check them out.

> Movement is good at any age. "The right music plays an important role in encouraging seniors to get more physical activity, which can help maintain independence and restore function lost due to injuries or illness," says the Elder Care Alliance.

Family Blog

Does your mother have a story or two to share? Maybe she has an opinion or two she feels strongly about—who doesn't? So, show her how we broadcast our personal opinions far and wide nowadays with a personal blog. Maybe she'll want a blog of her very own.

There are several free blogging platforms, all with extremely simple setup processes. Among the most popular are WordPress and Blogger. Help your mother decide by checking out both sites first to see if she can operate the basic template, and step back while she blogs away. . . .

Copy Cats

Is there a family habit or trait that you and your siblings all seem to share? Are you aware of the origins of the trait? It is high time you asked your mother why you all do the things you do. Write down a list of all of the things that you do unconsciously in the same way as your mother, and then ask why she did it that way. Do you all tie your shoes the same way? Have eggs for breakfast every morning? Could be that these are family habits that reach back into earlier generations and the lessons that have been passed on.

"In my family, no one refills the ice tray after it the ice has all been used—they put it back empty into the freezer! Drives me mad. And furthermore, my parents and my siblings leave the milk out on the counter during breakfast instead of putting it in the fridge between uses. Where did this all come from?"

—Gin Sander

Magical Mom Moments

Mom worked. My sisters and I didn't know what to think about it back in the fifties and sixties. None of our friends had working moms. Though we were very young, we were given many responsibilities. Of course, we complained about it all the time. The "King" and the "Queen" made us do all the work. We had to iron, dust, and vacuum on Wednesdays and help clean the house on Saturdays. We wrote a grocery list and bought the groceries. We learned to cook and had most dinners prepared and on the table by 5:30 p.m. We couldn't do anything until our responsibilities were done. That translated to deciding how much we wanted to do.

There was an upside. We had more freedom than some of our friends because we earned money. Five dollars a week would go very far in the 1960s. If Mom said that we were having a pot roast for dinner and I never cooked a pot roast before, I would bother neighbor ladies who were home and ask them to show me how to brown the meat, cut it apart, and put in just the right seasonings.

We didn't stop complaining until we left home. Then everything changed. We knew how to cook, clean, shop for groceries, do laundry then fold it. We baked fabulous desserts including cookies, many of which we invented. We set beautiful tables, carefully washing the china and silverware. Our friends thought we were amazing. They would tell stories about how we always had money for new shoes or to go to concerts and movies. And, we did.

Now we talk about how organized our mother was and how great it was to learn so much as kids. Her love, leadership, and organizational skills were handed down too. We were entrusted with managing our time and money. We never let her down. We call our mother the Original Super Mom because she was.

—Linda Nissen, Cathy MacHold, and Cyndi Geist-Tidd

su·per·mom
noun
INFORMAL·BRITISH

An exemplary or exceptional mother, especially one who successfully manages a home and brings up children while also having a full-time job.

"I'll be the first to admit that I am not supermom—I just can't do it all on my own."

—Unknown

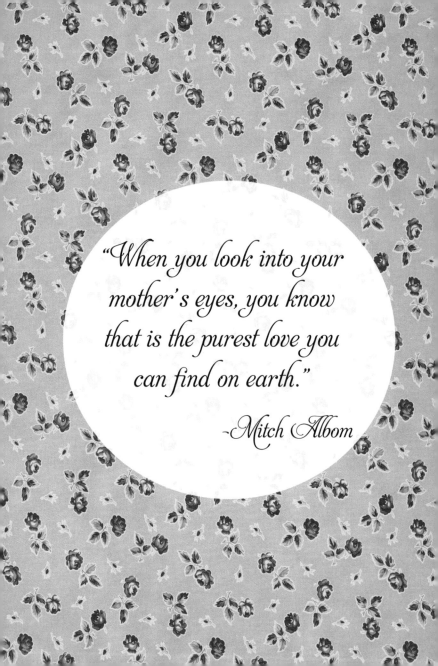

"When you look into your mother's eyes, you know that is the purest love you can find on earth."

-Mitch Albom

Offbeat Mama Movies

How about this as a fun way to spend a few hours together—watch an old movie with a motherhood theme. You could go the sentimental route with *Terms of Endearment*, *Steel Magnolias*, or *The Sound of Music*, or you could go for laughs with *Freaky Friday*. More recent offerings include Greta Gerwig's award-winning directorial debut, *Lady Bird*. The interplay and dialog between the mother and daughter is sometimes a tad too real, but chances are we can all relate, mothers and daughters alike.

Movie expert Matias Bombal of the Hollywood review site, mabhollywood.com, has more ideas on films to watch with your mother. His suggestions include *Mama Mia*, *Little Miss Sunshine*, *This is My Life*, and *Postcards from the Edge*.

Light Up My Life

John Harrison and Vanessa Whalen wanted a way to stay in touch with far-flung family and friends, to feel connected with folks spread around the country. They developed a product called a Friendship Lamp, which consists of two matching lamps that can be far from each other physically, but when one is touched, the matching lamp glows. Picture that—you live in one part of the country, your mother lives far away—but with these lamps in your homes you can each give the other a small little gesture of affection. The sight of the lamp in her home glowing because you touched yours in your home as you walked by is the equivalent of a small smile or glance in her direction. She will know you are thinking about her, even if you aren't physically there. Check them out on uncommongoods.com.

Framework

Not everything inside a frame needs to be artwork or a photo. Maybe you can frame the key to the first house your mother owned, or the christening dress that her mother wore? Shadow boxes are a wonderful way to highlight important family keepsakes. Wedding invitations, baby announcements—chances are that there are all kinds of mementos tucked around in your mother's house (or stashed in the attic) that would look great on the wall.

In addition to helping preserve family items by framing them, it is also a wonderful way to acknowledge the importance of seemingly ordinary items. Because we all want moments in our lives to be celebrated, and what better way than to frame them and hang them up for all to see?

Professional frames are an expensive undertaking, but keep an eye out for annual framing sales and the cost comes way down. Aaron Brothers, the framing section at the 1,200 Michael's craft stores around the country, has periodic sales that make it more affordable. Sign up to get their coupons and sales announcements.

"When someone asks you where you come from, the answer is your mother."

-Anna Quindlen

House Concerts

If your mother isn't interested in going out to hear music anymore, perhaps you can arrange for the music to come to her. House concerts are all the rage nowadays, where an independent musician performs in your living room in front of a group of friends and supporters. Sometimes the musicians are happy to just pass the hat afterwards, other times you can make it more formal and have a suggested donation to attend. One reason this movement has taken off is that it helps musicians get paid more directly, rather than losing a cut to a promoter. If you can gather thirty friends and family and they each pay twenty dollars, that gives the performer a healthy six hundred dollars for the night. They might also have CDs to sell, adding to the motivation to perform in your mother's living room.

How would you find a musician who wants to do a house concert? Ask any musician you know for local leads, or check out the website concertsinyourhome.org.

Magical Mom Moments

"Because I said so," my mother used to say, just before she dropped a cocktail onion in her glass. "Gibsons are better than martinis because I said so."

The drink is the same, as I'm sure you know. Gin (really expensive gin if your budget can handle it), a whisper of vermouth—truly just a whisper or perhaps merely a glance, or for the direst drink of all one just thinks briefly of adding vermouth and then realizes one's folly and moves on. Pure gin. Should anything else be added, though? A martini in the strictest sense has an olive. A Gibson has a cocktail onion. My mother is a Gibson Girl, my father a Martini Man. Late afternoon those two glass jars were always on the counter in the kitchen, olives and onions. As children we would dare each other to sniff the onion jar—*eww*—such a strong, sour smell.

My future as a gin drinker was determined early on, by the smell of a cocktail onion: not a chance. Olives weren't my love either, although I don't mind that green and red color scheme. Too sour and brackish, not to be touched. My own Martini Man likes to skewer three or four into his drink and call it dinner, but I am still eight years old when I catch a

whiff of cocktail olive and I still call it smelly. No, I opted early on for a twist of lemon. It smells good, looks crisp and healthy in the clear gin, not rancid like an olive or the creepy pale white onion floating corpse-like in your drink, either one cluttering up an otherwise good glass of gin. Defying your parents' ideas and striking out on your own is simply a part of growing up, and my path to adulthood started early, there at my parents' bar.

—Jennifer Basye Sander

Sunday Suppers

Was that a post-church tradition in your childhood? If so, perhaps it is time to revive it, regardless of whether there is still a church service involved. Because who doesn't like to sit at a big table surrounded by family and friends? Particularly if it isn't a big important holiday like Thanksgiving, Christmas, or Easter. Having a Sunday supper takes much of the pressure off of all involved as you don't have to worry about sticking to a traditional menu that everyone expects—and nobody can be disappointed if a classic is left off ("What? No pie? How could you!").

Butterfly Gardens

Is your mother a butterfly fan? Why not create a butterfly garden that will let her enjoy these magical beings all day long? There are many plants that attract butterflies, and just adding a few to a garden could make a real difference in the butterfly population that stop by to visit.

Best known is of course the Butterfly Bush, also known as buddleia. But in addition, you can plant poppies, cosmos, salvias, daisies, verbena, or liastris in any combination that appeals to you and your mother visually.

To attract magnificent Monarchs, you will need to plant milkweed. You should know, though, that there is a bit of controversy about the idea that there are year-round milkweed gardens. There is concern in the butterfly world that it adversely affects the traditional migratory patterns of the Monarchs.

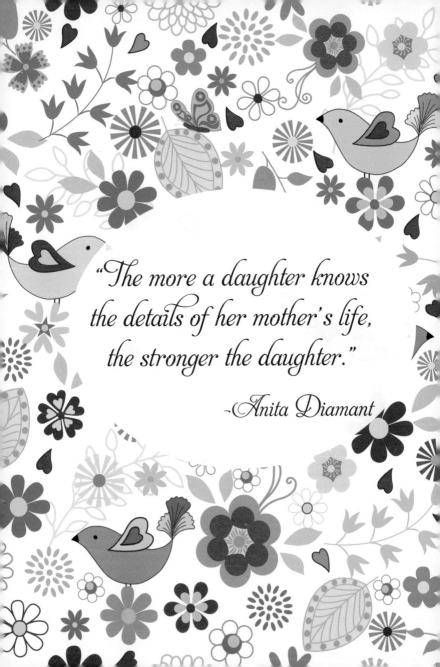

"The more a daughter knows the details of her mother's life, the stronger the daughter."

-Anita Diamant

A Sour Gift

Sourdough bread is delicious, and a loaf fresh out of the oven is pretty hard to beat. If your mother is a dedicated baker, perhaps she might like the gift of sourdough starter that you have made yourself. Even better if you create it from scratch by using wild yeast. Devotees of wild yeast say it includes health benefits that using store-bought yeast doesn't provide and is better for you both nutritionally and digestively.

You can find easy instructions for a basic sourdough starter at kingarthurflour.com, or go the wild yeast route with instructions you can find on weedemandreap.com.

Handmade Wreaths

S easonal wreaths are a lovely and welcoming touch on a front door. Your mother will think of you throughout the seasons if you make her a handmade wreath for her door or above the fireplace. Craft stores are filled with the supplies you need, just a simple foam, wire, or dried vine wreath form that you can decorate with fresh greenery and flowers from your own garden or hers.

Call Me

T*own & Country* magazine reports that more phone calls (approximately 122 million) are made on Mother's Day than any other day of the year. But really, why wait? Call because you just saw a vintage car on the road that reminds you of the old family car, call because you are standing in your kitchen making a recipe that she taught you, call because you just heard her favorite song playing as mood music in an elevator. You don't really need a reason. Call. Just call your mother.

Ever wonder why we say "Hello?" when we answer the phone? The standard greeting was sort of up in the air in the early days of the telephone. Alexander Graham Bell thought we should pick up a ringing phone and say, "Ahoy," as though we were hailing a passing ship. Thomas Edison is credited with promoting the idea of "hello," which comes from the British expression, "hullo."

Paper or Plastic?

You know the drill. Every store asks the question. Gone are the days when the grocery store bagger made the decision for you, and gone are the days when bags were free with purchase. So your mother needs her own bags to take to the grocery store! And you can make them for her, so that she takes you along with her in spirit, if not in person, whenever she goes.

The folks behind an organization called Morsbags encourage us all to stop using plastic bags for anything and make our own shopping bags from old bed sheets or curtains. Wouldn't it be a nice touch to make bags for your mother using curtains she loved so much she couldn't bear to throw them out? It is a great way to recycle sentimental fabrics she has been hanging on to.

For simple instructions on how to make a morsbag, visit morsbags.com

In Swedish, "mor" means mother. Morsbag would mean mother's bag, so perhaps there are some Swedes behind this movement. The website claims that so far close to 175,000,000 bags have been replaced through these efforts.

The Love List

Think back on the small things your mother did for you over the years . . . baking cookies, letting you choose the radio station, hemming your dress for the prom. Make a list and use that for a card, or send an email, or (gasp) write it out in an actual letter to send to your mother for no particular occasion.

We all too often overlook the ways that small gestures add up—the hundred or so times she drove you to swim team practice means you are a strong swimmer still; the breakfast she made for you every day in childhood means you still can't start your day unless you have a piece of raisin toast—so make a list of those small things and thank her for them. You'll be glad you did.

"We are born of love;
love is our mother."

-Rumi

Grade School Projects

Think back on all of the things you made for your mom when you were little, those homely projects from preschool and kindergarten. Did you make a plaque with your handprint in clay? Why not do it again, this time with your full-sized hand? It is certain to get a smile. Think about the projects your own children have been making and bringing home—the hand painted clay flower pot, the wooden frame with macaroni glued to it, a simple drawing—your own mother needs something to put in pride of place too, doesn't she? We think so!

Magical Mom Moments

My mom was the smartest woman I ever knew. I have thought so all my life. She was strong, often strong willed, beautiful, and funny with an aura of naivety. She didn't say needless things but meant what she said. Mom set the example. She was thoughtful and pensive and offered rare smart advice:

* Learn a skill that will provide you with a career
* Don't judge, understand
* Enjoy one day a week for a shared family meal
* Take care of a pet
* Make a homemade pie for Sunday dinner
* Don't go to bed angry
* Say your prayers, including others in your blessings
* Be grateful for what you have
* Don't spend money on needless things
* Don't catch a cold by leaving your laundry out at night
* Never marry the first person who asks
* Sex will take care of itself

I followed her advice and have offered it. My favorite, of course: "Enjoy one day a week for a shared family meal," added great value for my young family. Dinner conversations were a time for sharing, correcting, planning, and on one Thanksgiving holiday as the family gathered around the table, we shared what we were grateful for. Mom was in her late seventies then. My father had passed away earlier that year. The family joined hands, and each of us offered something like, "I'm grateful for good health" or "I'm grateful for my life," all good and heartfelt. Then we ended with Mom. "I am grateful for all of you," she started, "but it's because of me that you're all here." She said it slowly, looking at each of us.

We had never thought from the perspective of her practical statement before. There were several moments of silence as each of us soaked in her words. How true they were. As I watched my family, I noticed how my siblings looked at each other, husbands and wives re-assessed one another, how our children watched and listened. How true, the importance of us all, and we shared that moment in time all thinking the same thing: we wouldn't be here if it weren't for Mom (and Dad, of course).

Above all, enjoy one day a week for a shared family meal no matter how busy you are. If you are interested to read more, Dr. Anne K. Fishel's *Food for Thought* blog is a great place to start.

—Cathy MacHold

Classic Cooking

Julia Child's famed book *Mastering the Art of French Cooking* changed the way a generation of women cooked in the 1960s. In the 1970s, both *The Moosewood Cookbook* and Francis Moore Lappe's *Diet for a Small Planet* influenced the next group of women. In the 1980s, the two authors of *The Silver Palate* cookbooks had a hand in the dishes that hostesses cooked month after month (Chicken Marbella, anyone?). Did one of these cookbooks have an impact on the way your mother cooked? You'll never know unless you ask.

So go ahead and ask about her favorite cookbook, even if you think you already know the answer. How did she learn about it? From a friend or a television show? Possibly her own mother? Talking about cookbooks and recipes always sparks fond memories of beloved events, or perhaps of kitchen disasters that escaped your notice as a child.

Or another conversation sparking topic might be this—was there a cookbook or type of recipe she didn't like? Perhaps something her own mother-in-law urged her to cook? Once the conversation gets going you will of course have to haul the book down off the shelf to flip through and take a look at some of these recipes. And then you will have to cook them, with your own mother watching you carefully the entire time. . . .

"*Mother's love is peace, it need not be acquired, it need not be deserved.*"

-Erich Fromm

Magical Mom Moments

As I graduated from high school, my recently married sister, Linda, asked if I would come for a visit. It required a plane ticket to southern California and Mom agreed. I had never flown on an airplane. How wonderful to fly during the Golden Age of flying—I felt so grown-up. Mom offered to drive down and pick me up for the return trip. In the middle of my two sisters, I felt so special. She suggested that I take a summer school shorthand class to occupy my time as Linda worked during the day, and I agreed. After all, as mom would say, "Learn shorthand and you'll always be able to find employment." This was true and worthy advice in 1966.

During that summer I became restless and worried. I wasn't interested in shorthand or even working. My boyfriend and first love had been in a serious motorcycle accident and I didn't want to leave him. He was healing but I wouldn't be there for him. I wrote him daily and awaited his letters. One contained clippings of stitches within his words of love.

The time I shared with my sister was a gift and bonding experience. She was a woman now, married and living a coastal lifestyle, driving her Austin-Healey sports car with the top down, dropping me off at school. I was in awe of her. Time seemed to roll in and out measured by the daily mail.

Unbeknownst to her at the time, I was pregnant and afraid to talk about it. Though normally extroverted, I began to shut down. The options were frightening to me and I knew I didn't have a lot of time to mess with this. Mom and I talked on the phone, and I had many opportunities to share during the 580-mile drive back home—Mom had always been very open with me—but I could only stare out the window. At home, I went to bed but couldn't sleep. Still restless, I got up and went to our family room and to my surprise, Mom followed. She put her arms around me and asked in her normal loving voice, "What's the matter, Honey?" I told her. I'll always remember exactly what she said. "How are you feeling?" She wasn't angry, she didn't judge, she was Mom; my Mom, my loving, caring Mom.

As I think back on that time, perhaps Mom had her suspicions, hence the shorthand suggestion and the drive home. Mom and Linda probably had conversations about me that I was unaware of. Mom gave me the gift of time to sort through things and the place to do it. My story ends well. My boyfriend and I married and our precious Jennifer was born five months later. Every year on Jennifer's birthday she calls me and says, "Thanks for having me, Mom."

I never used my shorthand but I learned that life is full of surprises.

—Claire Manon

Build Your Mom a Library

You've seen those around, haven't you? The funny little book houses out in front of ordinary houses. Some look like the house itself, others are totally freeform, architecturally speaking. The whole Little Free Library movement grew out of one man's devotion to his mother. Todd Bol wanted to honor his late mother in some visible way, so he constructed a small replica of a one room schoolhouse and filled it with free books. A sign on the little structure urged passersby to either take a book or leave a book. From that one creative, loving effort, the Little Free Library movement sprang. There are now more than eighty thousand registered Little Free Libraries in ninety-one countries, and more pop up every day. Sadly, Bol died in 2018, but the non-profit organization he founded in 2009 to encourage others to make them lives on.

If your mom is an avid reader, just think of the fun she can have stocking her own library in front of the house. "I loved glancing out of my kitchen window and noticing someone stopped at my library," said Julia Berenson. "Nothing makes me happier than watching someone choose a book for themselves."

You can find out more information at littlefreelibrary.org.

Most Little Free Libraries are based on fairly simple designs available from the organization, but you can find more ideas in a new book, *Little Free Libraries and Tiny Sheds: 12 Miniature Structures You Can Build*, by Philip Schmidt.

Memory Questions

Sometimes it can be hard to get a conversation going with a parent. And sometimes we are all too focused on the daily here and now to move the conversation into a place where we might learn new information about each other. Try some of these questions to begin a more far-ranging conversation with your mother:

- Do you have a favorite memory of your own mother?

- What was your favorite outfit in high school? Where did it come from? Did you make it yourself?

- Did you have an imaginary career when you were daydreaming? Scientist? Fashion model? Diplomat?

- What world event has had the biggest impact on your life?

- Is there something that you wish you could do over again?

Contributors

Kathryn Canan inherited her parents' love of music, travel, and education. A Montana native, she majored in biochemistry and then, predictably, became an early music specialist. She enjoys performing and teaching music of all periods on historical flutes, recorders, and whistles. She lives in California's gold country in the Sierra foothills, enjoying the modern-day riches of the foothill arts culture.

Susan Dlugach has worked in libraries, a liquor store, a bank, has been a journalist, and is an English teacher. She currently lives in Sacramento, California, with her family and kitty, Feliz.

Nina Foster is a Farmer Florist and jewelry designer. She enjoys sharing her passions doing event work and teaching. She creates treasures with an earthy feel. Nina lives with her family in Skagit Valley, Washington. You can find her jewelry and wreaths on trilliumfinch.com

Donnella (Ella) Fradkin started out as a singer/songwriter in Los Angeles, where she fell in love with comedy and began writing and performing her material regularly at places like the Comedy Store on Sunset, the Improv, and the Ice House. Today she calls Sacramento home, where she shares her passion for writing and performs short stories and songs about her life changing experiences.

Rose Ann Goodwin recently retired from a career as a corporate administrator to focus on her writing. She began writing stories and poetry in her early teens and enjoys writing creative nonfiction. Between her love of nature and her large, eclectic family, she has more material than she could possibly use in a lifetime. Rose Ann is currently working on a novel about her older brother who she spent her high school years loving and hating through his struggles as a heroin addict.

JT Long has written for books, magazines, websites, and once on a gas station bathroom wall, but only because there was a grammar mistake on the sign and she happened to have a red pen handy.

Ingrid Lundquist is a creative spirit. After a career as a Certified Special Events Professional, she took up photography in 2011 and since then has been in more than seventy juried shows across the US and abroad. She is the founder of The Book-in-Hand Roadshow which stages presentations and workshops on topics of interest to writers. She is the author of three business books on event production, a photo story book, and two books related to self-publishing.

Cathy MacHold, author of *Writing with Hemingway: A Writer's Exercise Book*, is an Independent Hemingway Scholar and a presenter at two Hemingway Society conferences—including the IVII International Hemingway Conference in Paris, where she presented her paper, *Oh, Those Hemingway Clothes* at the American University. Cathy is also the co-curator of "The Veneto Photos" collection shown in various locations during 2019 to commemorate Hemingway's 120th birthday. Cathy designed a series of Pathway Culinary 101 classes to help adult students "get hired" and teaches other creative culinary classes.

Ken MacHold followed a successful career in law enforcement as a District Attorney Investigator with a career as a private investigator. His writings include investigative reports. He owns a small vineyard, where he tends and makes his own wine. Ken is the proud winner of a bronze medal at the California State Fair in 2019, from his first harvest, a 2017 Cabernet Franc. Ken is an avid world traveler, kayaker, and skier who enjoys sharing time with his family and friends.

Dr. Carey Clements Rote is a professor of art history at Texas A&M University, Corpus Christi. She is a popular speaker on art and history and has taught art history to generations of young, aspiring artists. The professor is an expert in Pre-Colombian and Guatemalan art who also specializes in Day of the Dead art, Chicano art, and Mexican colonial art. She has presented papers across the nation, in Costa Rica, Mexico, and Macedonia. Dr. Rote taught a summer course in Florentine Art for Santa Reparata School of the Arts in Florence, Italy.

Nancy Weaver Teichert is a retired award-winning newspaper reporter and serves on the board of the Community of Writers at Squaw Valley. She and her husband of twenty-eight years live in Sacramento, California, as do her three stepdaughters and their families. Her six grandchildren call her Nana.

Wendy Watson was a psychotherapist for twenty-five years and is now retired. She loves to backpack, weave, and write. She lives with her husband in Davis, California, and has a son.